# Lunch in Space

written by Kana Riley

illustrated by Michael Chesworth

HARCOURT BRACE & COMPANY

Orlando Atlanta Austin Boston San Francisco Chicago Dallas New York
Toronto London

Welcome!
We're having lunch in space.

It's not the same as lunch on Earth.
We'll show you how we do it.

3

First we have to take out the trays and stick them on the wall.

If we don't stick them on the wall, they will float away in space.

We take out the hot dogs,
open the oven door,
and put them in to cook.

If we don't do these things in space, the food will float away.

We mix water and orange powder to make the orange drink. The boxes fit in the trays.

It's a good thing
because even drinks
can float away in space.

Come and get it!
Everybody takes a tray

and finds a seat—
on the wall,
or on the ceiling.

Yes, even people will float away up here!

13

It's a good lunch.

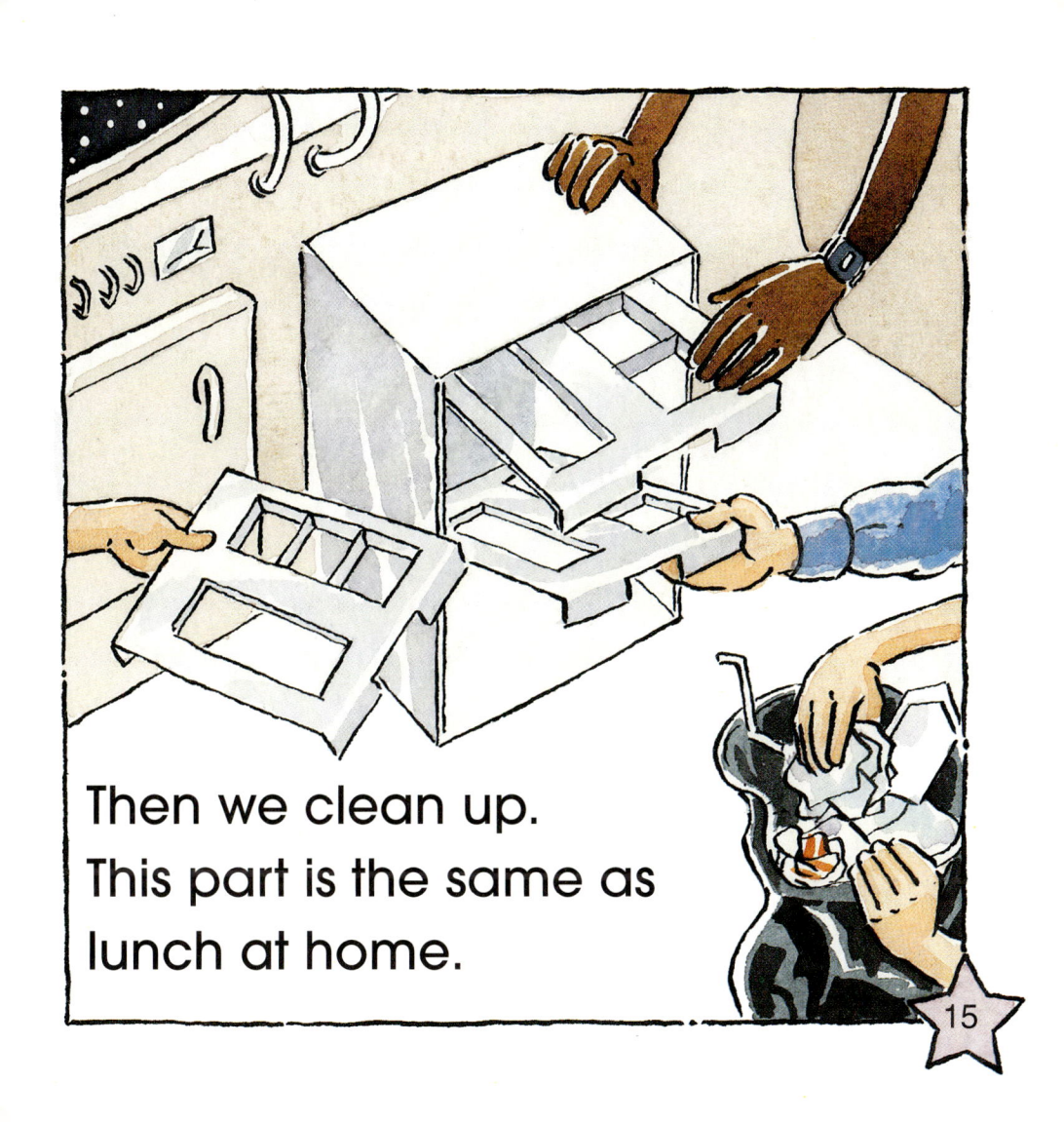

Then we clean up.
This part is the same as lunch at home.

Well, not quite like home!